STUDY GUIDE

GOD'S
ARMOR
BEARER
VOLUMES 1 & 2
Serving God's Leaders

D1276903

STUDY GUIDE

GOD'S
ARMOR
BEARER
VOLUMES 1 & 2
Serving God's Leaders

TERRY NANCE

Unless otherwise indicated, all Scripture quotations are taken from the King James Version of the Bible.

Armorbearer Study Guide
ISBN 0-97191-933-X
Copyright © 2003 by Terry Nance

Published by Focus on the Harvest
P.O. Box 241546
Little Rock, Arkansas 72223

Contents

The Bible states that many are called, but few are chosen. Becoming the chosen of God is a choice on your part to pray, to live in faith, integrity, diligence, and excellence of ministry. You must determine to have those attributes in your life and to be committed to the will of God no matter the cost.

God's armorbearers are God-called ministers, chosen and sent by the Spirit of God to assist leadership with the vision He has placed within them. These armorbearers take the load off the officer and help to impart his or her vision into the people. These New Testament armorbearers are intensely loyal, faithful, and service-motivated people. They serve as bodyguard, friend, companion, confidant, spiritual warrior, and many other roles as the list of service is interminable. The position of the armorbearer is one that requires great love, honor, tolerance, and watchfulness.

That is why this study guide is a vital element in the *God's Armorbearer* series. There is no right way or wrong way to use this study guide. You may complete the exercises in the privacy of your home, or you can use it in a group setting or with a partner. The only condition is that you read the chapters from the *God's Armorbearer* book that the study guide relates to so that you can gain further insight and understanding about your role as an armorbearer. The guide serves to illuminate and highlight many of the statements in the book. As you begin the exercises, pray and ask God to open your eyes and give you understanding so that you can fulfill your calling. Follow through each exercise, researching the words, completing the activities, and opening your heart for instruction, correction, and encouragement. Remember, the spirit of the armorbearer is the Spirit of Christ. The armorbearers of today will be the leaders of tomorrow. Enjoy the journey!

Part One

–1–

Revelation of an Armorbearer

The Old Testament describes the lives of several armor-bearers and their leaders. The last armorbearer story is found in First Samuel 16:14-23.

1. Who are those scriptures referring to?_____

2. According to those scriptures, name six characteristics that were found in this armorbearer.

a. _____

_____

b. _____

_____

c. _____

_____

d. _____

_____

e. _____

_____

f. _____

3. We live in a world that seems to know very little about laying down one's life for another. Why is that is true?

_____

_____

_____

_____

4. List some areas where you can change this type of attitude in your own life.

a. _____

_____

b. _____

_____

c. _____

_____

d. _____

_____

e. _____

Let's Go To Bible School

You'll need a concordance for this one! (We recommend a Strong's Concordance.)

5. The word armorbearer is listed 18 times in the Old Testament. Using a concordance, list the scripture references for the word, armorbearer.

_____

_____

_____

_____

6. In the Stong's concordance, there are two reference numbers that define the Hebrew interpretation of the word armorbearer. What are those two Hebrew words?

a. _____

_____

b. _____

_____

7. What does the first primary word mean?

_____

_____

8. What are the applications of the first primary Hebrew word?

_____

_____

9. According to Chapter 1, what is the meaning of the second primary word?

_____

_____

10. What are the applications for the use of the second word?

_____

_____

_____

11. From these two Hebrew words and using my analogy in Chapter 1, what was the overall duty of the armorbearer?

_____

_____

_____

12. The spirit of an armorbearer is the _____ of _____. It is the _____ of a _____.

–2–

Function of an Armorbearer

Just for fun, I want you to take a private test. If you are in a study group, you don't have to show your answers. The purpose of this test is for you to locate what is truly in your heart and help you realize what you need to work on when it comes to serving God through serving His leaders. As you read each statement, circle where your attitude rates on a scale from 1 to 4 (1 being the worst and 4 being the best). Be honest!

When my leaders ask me to do something, I always do it with a cheerful heart.

     1   2   3   4

If I don't agree with a leader, I think I should argue my point.

     1   2   3   4

When I see a leader, I cringe inside and want to hide.

     1   2   3   4

I battle with thoughts like, "Who does they think they are?"

     1   2   3   4

I usually compete with leadership, wanting the people to know exactly what I did.

    1   2   3   4

I'm obedient to do what I'm asked, but I talk about the leader when he/she is not around.

    1   2   3   4

I shift the pressure of off myself by stating, "Pastor wants this."

    1   2   3   4

If I had been David, I would have killed Saul when I had the chance!

    1   2   3   4

There are no right or wrong answers – just attitude adjustments where necessary! If you find an attitude rating that you aren't pleased with, work on it, pray about it, and saturate yourself with scriptures pertaining to it.

Although reference material which would allow us to investigate the procedure of how an armorbearer was chosen is not available, it is obvious that the position was one of heartfelt loyalty. It is also obvious that the armorbearer was much more than just a hired hand – he was chosen and selected by the officer he would serve. Unquestioning obedience was absolutely necessary, although after a few years, the armorbearer probably did not need to be told what his officer was thinking – he knew his officer as he knew himself.

Chapter 2 lists eleven duties of an armorbearer. Let's discuss each duty.

First Duty

1. To be an armorbearer, you must provide _____ for your leader.

   A. By his very presence, a true armorbearer will always display and produce an attitude of _____ and _____.

   B. Why are the attitudes of faith and peace important if you are to be successful in service as an armorbearer?

_____

_____

_____

_____

_____

2. It will minister to your pastor if he can sense the _____ and _____, which is an integral part of your lifestyle.

3. It is a great relief to the pastor to know that he does not have to carry his armorbearer _____, _____ and _____.

Second Duty

1. An armorbearer must have a deep-down sense of
_____ for his leader, and _____ for,
and _____ of, his leader's
_____ and his way of doing things.

Let's Talk About It

1. Do you believe God made us all with different personalities?

_____

_____

_____

2. Are personalities important?   If so, why?

_____

_____

_____

3. Do you think life would be better if we all had the same personality?

_____

_____

_____

4. In your opinion, what is the difference between a personality quirk and a detrimental personality?

In your opinion, when do personality conflicts become

detrimental to a ministry?

_____

_____

_____

2. Since God made us with different personalities, at least fifty percent of the time, your pastor's way of doing things will differ from yours. Should that difference be allowed to cause a problem for you or your spiritual leader?

_____

   A. Be honest! Even if you wanted to answer yes, then list the reasons why a personality difference would cause problems between you and your pastor.

_____

_____

_____

   B. Now take each of the reasons that you have listed and lay them before the Lord. Ask Him to help you overcome petty personality differences and to give you eyes to see the spiritual goal ahead for you instead of the conflict around you.

_____

_____

_____

3. I learned a secret that helped me flow in harmony with my pastor, and that secret will help you too. What is it?

_____

_____

_____

4. Our _____ is the same, our _____ differ.

5. What does the above statement mean to you?

_____

_____

_____

6. If you will adopt this attitude toward your pastor, there will be a knitting of hearts between the two of you. Your pastor will know that you are not there to _____ with him/her or to _____ his/her decisions, but that you are there to _____ him/her in achieving his God-given objectives.

Third Duty

1. To be an armorbearer, you must instinctively understand your leader's _____.

2. Read each statement below and determine whether it is true (T) or false (F). When you are finished, check your answers with those in the answer key at the back of this study guide.

a. I should complain to my pastor about our differences.

   T   F

b. I must not be in the right place if we don't think alike.

   T   F

c. It only took a day for the disciples to think like Jesus.

   T   F

d. God's Spirit was eventually imparted into the disciples.

   T   F

e. After a period of time, your pastor's spirit will come upon you.

   T   F

f. When your pastor's spirit is upon you, you will think like he/she thinks.

   T   F

Let's Switch Roles

For just a moment, imagine you are the pastor or leader. God has given you an assignment. You know what He expects, you know the obstacles and you know the goals you have set to get there. Now, imagine the people surrounding you that have come to be armorbearers to you. How would it feel if:

They challenged your authority in getting the job done?

They challenged your way of attaining the goals?

They consistently thought their way was better?

They criticized your motives or procedures?

Sometimes when we switch roles with each other, it is easier for us to discover and confess our agreement. Begin to say now, "In Jesus' name, I understand how my pastor thinks and I flow with him/her in the spirit of understanding!"

Talk It Out

We are all unique individuals, designed by God with personalities, motivations, gifts and callings. If two people were placed in a room, they would each have a difference of opinions, ideas, and convictions. That may be why the Word says if two or more can agree, great power would occur! As an armorbearer, it's not a sin to have a different opinion, a different idea, or a different conviction from your leader. In fact, you can count on it. That's why communication is so important and the way you communicate is so vital. For example, God gave us His Word to communicate what He expects from us and why. We should always seek to have relationships that communicate, or there will be misunderstanding and offense.

3. If there are times when you are troubled or confused about what your leader has asked you to do, then communication is a must. You have a right to approach your leader with a teachable and humble spirit, and simply ask the questions you need answers to. Below are scriptures that will keep your heart prepared for effective, respectful communication, even when you disagree.

a. Write out First Timothy 5:1

_____

_____

b. What does that verse mean to you?

_____

_____

_____

c. Write out First Thessalonians 5:12,13.

_____

_____

_____

_____

d. What do these verses mean to you?

_____

_____

_____

If you keep your heart prepared, you will know how to communicate honorably. Here are some examples of how to open the doors of communication.

"I need to understand why you are approaching the task in this manner so I can fulfill what God has called me to do beside you."

"I need your help in this way. To troubleshoot the task and cause it to operate smoothly, can you ... (explain what you need and why). "

By always using terms like, "I need" and "I feel," the communication is open, respectful, honest, and non-threatening. Remember, communication is the key to successful relationships!

Fourth Duty

1. To be an effective armorbearer, you must walk in
_____ with and _____ to your
leader.

2. In order to be an armorbearer, you must have Romans
13:1,2 settled in your heart. Write the two verses below.

_____

_____

_____

_____

3. Write what these two verses mean to you.

_____

_____

_____

4. The word submit means to "retire, withdraw, yield, and
obey."1 How does the definitions of that word apply to the
way you submit to those in authority?

_____

_____

_____

5. Read First Peter 5:5. Below are statements pertaining to
this scripture. Circle whether the statement is true (T) or
false (F). Check your answers in the back of the book.

a. "Younger" can mean spiritually, physically, or mentally.

T   F

b. The only exception to this command is a directive that violates Scripture.

T   F

c. If a directive violates Scripture, you must obey the higher authority – God.

T   F

d. The "higher authority" is always God's Word.

T   F

6. Matthew 5:3, 5, 7-9 describes five core attitudes that believers must have to walk in submission. What are those five attributes?

_____

_____

_____

_____

_____

7. These five attributes will cause you to submit willingly and cheerfully, not only to God but also to others in authority as well.

Look up the following words in the dictionary and write the definitions. Based on the definitions, examine your personal behavior and thoughts. Be honest and grow!

A. Humble / Humility:

_____

_____

How have you demonstrated this attribute in the past week?

_____

_____

How have you fallen short of it?

_____

_____

How can you improve in this area?

_____

_____

B. Meek:

_____

_____

How have you demonstrated this attribute in the past week?

_____

_____

How have you fallen short of it?

_____

_____

How can you improve in this area?

_____

_____

C. Forgive:

_____

_____

How have you demonstrated this attribute in the past week?

_____

_____

How have you fallen short of it?

_____

_____

How can you improve in this area?

_____

_____

D. Purity:

_____

_____

How have you demonstrated this attribute in the past week?

_____

_____

How have you fallen short of it?

_____

_____

How can you improve in this area?

_____

_____

E. Conscience (clear):

_____

_____

How have you demonstrated this attribute in the past week?

_____

_____

How have you fallen short of it?

_____

_____

How can you improve in this area?

_____

_____

What Are You Following

Based on the information in Chapter 2, circle the correct answer.

8. You must submit to your pastor the same way you_____.

a. Pay your bills.

b. Surrender the TV remote to your mate.

c. Agree to mow the lawn.

d. Submit to Jesus.

9. Refusing to submit to God's delegated authority is_____.

a. Refreshing.

b. Exciting.

c. Refusing to submit to God.

d. True manliness.

10. If a person claims to be submitted to God, then the person is _____.

a. A nun.

b. Submitted to God's delegated authority.

c. Looking for God in Mother Earth.

d. Ready to start their ministry.

11. When we obey, we do not submit to the individual himself but _____.

a. To the paycheck he gives us.

b. To the corporation that employs us.

c. To God's authority in him.

d. To eventually get his position.

12. When we submit, we must not look at the person,

but_____.

a. At the office he occupies.

b. At the prosperity he has.

c. At all the big names he knows.

d. At how much he pays us.

13. When we submit, we do not regard the man, but
_____.

a. The position.

b. The salary.

c. The "meeting" if we don't.

d. Ladder of success we want to climb.

14. Anything less than full submission is _____
_____.

a. Rebellion.

b. Full control.

c. Holding on to your dignity.

d. A person who knows who they are.

15. God will never establish you as an authority until you have first learned to _____.

a. Honor other cultures.

b. Open the door for your wife.

c. Sit through a NASCAR race.

d. Submit to authority.

Fifth Duty

1. An armorbearer must make the _____ of his leader his most important goal.

Just A Thought

A. Think about how Jesus sacrificed His own desires in order to fulfill the Father's will. List some of the ways here.

_____

_____

_____

_____

B. Remember, if you will have the same attitude and serve God by serving others, God will exalt you, no matter what circumstances you may face!

Sixth Duty

1. An armorbearer must possess endless strength so as to
_____, _____ and _____ his
way onward without giving way under harsh treatment.

How does the dictionary define the words below?

A. Thrust: _____

_____

B. Press:_____

_____

C. Force: _____

_____

2. How have you had to use this kind of spiritual strength
in serving leadership?

_____

_____

3. How did it benefit you and the cause you were working
toward?

_____

_____

4. Was there a time when you failed to use this spiritual
strength and suffered for it?

What are your thoughts about that now?

_____

_____

5. Write out First Peter 2:20.

_____

_____

_____

6. What does this verse mean to you?

_____

_____

_____

7. Read First Samuel 30:6. When the battle is raging against you, how do you encourage yourself in the Lord?

_____

_____

8. What are some other ways that you would like to encourage yourself in the Lord?

_____

_____

Attitude Check!

First Peter 2:20 makes it very clear that there will be times in the midst of the battle when we feel we are being wrongfully treated. These times are bound to arise, but do not allow Satan to put resentment into your heart.

Read each statement below and based on the information in Chapter 2, circle the answer that best fits the situation. Check your answers at the back of the book.

9. If you have done right, yet instead you are being wrongfully treated, _____.
   a. Learn to give the situation over to the Lord and patiently endure.
   b. Call the local newspaper and trash the pastor.
   c. Nurse it and rehearse it until you know it by heart.
   d. Tell all of your friends so they will stop attending the church.

10. If you learn to patiently endure, _____.
   a. You are a fool.
   b. God will be pleased with you.
   c. You like to be taken advantage of.
   d. You are a weak person.

11. If you think your decision was right, but the leader thinks it was wrong, those situations produce _____.
   a. Crying that never stops.
   b. Huge arguments.
   c. Godly character—if you walk in love.
   d. Lasting friendships.

12. When you are rebuked for what is right, the easiest thing to do is _____.

a. Go to Baskin Robbins and have an ice cream.

b. Get into a fight with your mate.

c. Quit.

d. To tell the pastor what you think of him/her.

13. When you are stinging from a rebuke, the best thing to do is _____.

a. To call your mother.

b. To call your best friend with all the horrible details.

c. Lock your door and refuse to answer the phone.

d. Pray until the victory comes.

14. In Psalm 34:1, David loudly proclaimed _____.

a. "Break their teeth, O God!"

b. "Let their way be dark and slippery."

c. "Lord, how long wilt thou look on?"

d. "I will bless the Lord at all times."

Seventh Duty

1. An armorbearer must follow orders _____
   and _____.

2. In order to be a good leader, you must be a good follow-
   er. Let's take a fun quiz to see if you are on the road to
   becoming a good leader. Look at the chart below. Across
   the top are six letters that correspond to six statements.
   Read the first statement. Now look at the first column
   marked A. On a scale of 1 to 8 (8 being the highest – "I
   always do this; always feel this way" and 1 being the lowest – "I never do this; never feel this way"), rate yourself.
   Once you have answered the questions, draw a line
   between the numbers you have circled, connecting the
   columns. Answer honestly!

A	B	C	D	E	F
8	8	8	8	8	8
7	7	7	7	7	7
6	6	6	6	6	6
5	5	5	5	5	5
4	4	4	4	4	4
3	3	3	3	3	3
2	2	2	2	2	2
1	1	1	1	1	1

A. Whenever I'm told to do something, I take care of it
   quickly and efficiently.

B. I feel that the one I serve knows I can be totally depend-
   ed upon to carry out his/her directives.

C. I write down the orders I'm given to make sure the
   leader gets exactly what he/she asked for.

D. If I don't understand, I ask for an explanation to make sure I have the correct information.

E. I have never misrepresented my leader because I have never misunderstood what he/she meant.

F. I treat my orders with high priority, putting my whole heart into it.

Notice the line you have drawn to connect the columns. Is it jagged? Is it a smooth line, running straight across? How jagged is your road to becoming a good leader? Are there areas that need some tightening up? If you answered honestly, this test will show you where those areas are!

Eighth Duty

1. An armorbearer must be a _____ to his leader.

2. According to the definition in Chapter 2, what does the word supporter mean?

   _____

   _____

3. Contrary to popular belief, pastors are human. List some ways this is true.

   _____

   _____

4. How does the armorbearer's job as supporter help the pastor?

   _____

   _____

5. Do we have too many babies in the Body of Christ? What defines a spiritual baby?

   _____

   _____

6. When is the only time that an armorbearer is called to be out in front of the pastor?

   _____

   _____

7. When do you begin to make real progress towards becoming a leader?

   _____

   _____

Ninth Duty

1. An armorbearer must be an excellent _____.

2. Read the statements below and circle the correct answer whether true (T) or false (F). Check your answers at the back of the book.

a. If you want a good relationship, communication is the most important thing.
   T   F

b. Communication is the only way to build trust between the pastor and you.
   T   F

c. Make the pastor aware of what is going on in the church and with the people.
   T   F

d. Never hide anything from your pastor.
   T   F

e. If someone is causing trouble, tell the pastor what you are doing to resolve it.
   T   F

f. You owe it to your leader to reveal anything that will cause problems.
   T   F

g. Secrecy is a trap that Satan lays for the unsuspecting.

    T   F

h. Mark 4:22 says that nothing is hidden that will not be revealed.

    T   F

i. If someone asks you not to share certain information with your pastor, then don't.

    T   F

Tenth Duty

1. An Armorbearer must have a _____ that will eagerly gain _____ for his leader.

2. A true armorbearer will always strive to _____ his pastor well before all men.

3. What did David say of the Lord in Second Samuel 22:36?

   _____

   _____

4. What are some ways that you can be aware of how you represent your leader and your church?

   _____

   _____

   _____

5. What are some examples of someone trying to save his/her own reputation at the expense of the pastor's reputation?

   _____

   _____

6. Even though you are not the shepherd of the flock, as an armorbearer, you must take into your spirit the

   _____ _____ ____ _____.

7. In dealing with people, what are some ways to take on the heart of a shepherd?

_____

_____

_____

8. Again, what are the five core attributes for a good armorbearer?

_____

_____

_____

_____

_____

Eleventh Duty

1. An armorbearer must have the ability to minister _____ and _____ to his leader.

2. According to Chapter 2, what is the definition of courage?

   _____

   _____

3. List some times when courage was required of you.

   _____

   _____

4. Read the account in Numbers 13 where the spies were sent into the Promised Land. Out of twelve men, how many had the courage to obey God and possess it?

   a. _____

5. b. What were their names?

   _____

   _____

5. Courage comes from _____ in God.

6. In order to minister in the same assurance as your pastor has, you must stay built up in the _____

   _____ _____.

7. In serving on the staff of a ministry, what is one deception

that must be guarded against?

_____

_____

8. Complete this sentence. The vision of the church you are called to serve is God's vision, and if He did not think you could fit in with it, _____

_____

_____

9. You will not always get a pat on the back for doing a good job. Why? Because as Christians, our rewards are

_____

10. Your rewards in heaven will be determined by your _____ here and now on this earth.

–3–

Armorbearers of the Old Testament

1. **Read** Judges 9:45-55. Tell in your own words the story of Abimelech and his armorbearer.

   _____

   _____

   _____

   _____

2. Based on what you have already learned about an armorbearer, name the qualities that you find in Abimelech's armorbearer.

   _____

   _____

   _____

   _____

3. Read First Samuel 31:4-6 and First Chronicles 10:4-5. Tell the story of Saul and his armorbearer in your own words.

   _____

   _____

   _____

   _____

4. Why wouldn't Saul's armorbearer trust him with the sword?

_____

_____

_____

5. How did Saul's armorbearer die and why did it happen?

_____

_____

_____

6. Read First Samuel 14:1-23. Tell of the story in your own words.

_____

_____

_____

7. List three classic examples of the humility and diligence that Jonathan's armorbearer displayed.

_____

_____

_____

8. Read again, First Samuel 16:14-23. Tell the story in your own words.

_____

_____

_____

_____

9. Verse 18 listed six qualities that young David had as an

armorbearer. What were they?

_____

_____

_____

_____

10. In First Samuel 26:9, David stated that he would not touch God's anointed. Why did he say that?

_____

_____

_____

Who's Who?

Match the correct armorbearer with the correct story. Answers are in the back of the book.

A. Abimelech's armorbearer

B. Saul's armorbearer

C. Jonathan's armorbearer

D. Young David

1. _____ He answered, "Do all that you have in mind...Go ahead! I am with you heart and soul."

2. _____ He was asked to kill his leader so that that the enemy would not capture him.

3. _____ This armorbearer never struck back, no matter how many times his leader tried to kill him.

4. _____ This armorbearer cut off the edge of his leader's

robe and was sorrowful about it.

5. _____ This armorbearer killed his leader for reputation's sake.

6. _____ After his leader committed suicide, this armorbearer took his own life as well.

7. _____ He stayed after his leader, slaying the enemy that had been knocked to the ground.

8. _____ He could not kill his leader because of being "sore afraid."

–4–

New Testament Armorbearing

1. There are significant differences between the armorbearers of the Old Testament and the armorbearers of the New Testament. Below are statements found in Chapter 4. At the end of each statement, answer whether it is true (T) or false (F). Answers are at the back of the book.

A. In OT days, the duty of an armorbearer was the number one priority.

   T   F

B. In NT days, the duty of an armorbearer is still the number one priority.

   T   F

C. Although physical duties have changed, the attitude of the heart is the same.

   T   F

D. The position of an armorbearer is one that God calls for a short time.

   T   F

E. The armorbearer position is not a "stepping stone" position.

   T   F

F. You should always ask God if the current position is one He has chosen for you.

   T   F

G. A close personal relationship is not necessary to be a good armorbearer.

   T   F

H. As an armorbearer, you are called to serve a general of God's army.

    T   F

I. An armorbearer's purpose is to pull down strongholds for pastor, church, and city.

    T   F

J. Both with OT and NT armorbearers, the main function is combat.

    T   F

K. In the OT, armorbearer combat was physical; in the NT, combat is spiritual.

    T   F

L. There is no "second fiddle" position in the Body of Christ.

    T   F

M. New Testament Armorbearing is a ministry of prayer, watchfulness, and intercession.

    T   F

Although the word armorbearer is not mentioned in the New Testament, we can see from the scriptures that the attitude and spirit of an armorbearer is found throughout the pages of the New Covenant.

2. Read the scripture references below. As a NT armorbearer, think about your life as you serve the leader God has placed you with. Write what these scripture references mean to you.

A. Matthew 18:1-4.

_____

_____

_____

B. John 15:13.

_____

_____

_____

C. Ephesians 6:5,6.

_____

_____

_____

D. Philippians 2:3-9.

_____

_____

_____

E. First Thessalonians 5:12,13.

_____

_____

_____

F. First Peter 5:5, 2:20.

_____

_____

Laying Down the Foundation

3. God has a set order in the way He builds the Body of Christ and the Church. Below are statements that are jumbled and out of sequence. You must put these statements in order – just the way God sets the Church in order! Write the correct number order (what comes first, second, third, and so on) beside the statement.

_____The Lord sends God-called ministers to assist the man/woman of God and to take his/her spirit upon them.

_____God places His vision inside of a person and His anointing upon him/her to carry it forth.

_____These people act as armorbearers; their function is to take the load off their officer and to help impart the vision into the people.

_____God will surround that individual with other people who will support and work with him/her toward the fulfillment of that vision.

'X' Marks the Truth

4. The statements below contain armorbearer truths and fallacies. Based on the information in Chapter 4, now it's your job to determine the true from the false. Place an "X" by the true characteristics of an armorbearer.

A. _____ Strives to keep his godly priorities in line.

B. _____ Wants to have dinner with the pastor every Friday night.

C. _____ Aids his leader in spiritual combat.

D. _____ Serves his leader well, expecting no reward from man, but knowing that Jesus will reward him one day for his efforts and loyalty.

E. _____ Called to be his pastor's fishing buddy.

F. _____ Goal is to get next to the pastor.

H. _____ Sees his position as one called and instituted by God.

−5−

The Cry of God's Leaders

1. **The** number one question leaders must ask themselves:
   Are you willing to be a Moses to your Joshua?

2. List some ways a leader might "invest" into the life of
   another.

   _____

   _____

   _____

3. According to Chapter 5, there are truths that leaders
   must realize to see that his/her ministry belongs to God,
   not to them. What are those truths?

   _____

   _____

   _____

4. Fill in the blanks to list the four basic principles that every
   leader must look for in finding a "Joshua" for their ministry.

   a. _____ for God's _____-_____ people to come your way.

   b. Be willing to _____ _____ in the lives of your
   helpers.

c. _____ authority. (Remember: If you are going to give anyone _____ in any area, then be big enough to give him/her the _____ he/she needs to carry it out.)

d. Look for the _____ of an _____ in people.

5. As a leader looking for armorbearers, be sure to ask yourself this question: What good is a _____ without an _____ to follow him?

–6–

How to Develop the Spirit of an Armorbearer

The spirit of an armorbearer doesn't just happen. The armorbearer spirit comes by the decision on your part to become the chosen of God, giving full attention to the details of your life. There are four major areas in which we need to judge ourselves in order to break Satan's power in our lives so that we can be pleasing to God and be a light in the world.

1. List those 4 major areas by which Satan tries to hinder us.

a. _____

b. _____

c. _____

d. _____

How do you know if you are hindered in one or several of these areas? Let's take a test. Read the statements below. On a scale from 1 to 4 (with 1 being the lowest and 4 the highest), circle the number rating how well the statement describes you. Now this test takes sheer honesty on your part. Remember, the goal is to discover and then to be set free so that we can be all God wants us to be! When you are finished with the test, check your answers at the end to see the areas in which you are being hindered.

Section 1

I don't want to go to a church meeting if it's on a subject I've heard many times.

    1   2   3   4

I don't want to submit to a man, but I will submit to God.

    1   2   3   4

I have a strong will and if God doesn't help me immediately, I will do it myself.

    1   2   3   4

I am pleased I have a strong will and I let everyone know about it.

    1   2   3   4

I would rather show that I am sorry for something instead of apologizing for it.

    1   2   3   4

It's easier to do it myself rather than trust someone else to take care of it.

    1   2   3   4

I know exactly how I want something done, and I don't think it's wrong to say so.

    1   2   3   4

If I know about a subject, I'll make sure that everyone knows I do.

    1   2   3   4

I'm easier on my own mistakes than I am toward the mistakes of others.

    1   2   3   4

No matter what someone has been through, I have a story like it that I have to tell.

    1   2   3   4

I caught myself snarling at a woman with a short skirt and a cigarette.

    1   2   3   4

I always want to be the center of attention – my position requires it.

    1   2   3   4

If my beliefs are challenged, I get angry

    1   2   3   4

I think it brings respect if I tell people about the great things I've done or who I know

    1   2   3   4

It's a sign of weakness to lower myself and help others on a consistent basis.

    1   2   3   4

Success means doing whatever I want and knowing God will be with me.

    1   2   3   4

I am secretly happy when others around me fail because it makes me look better.

    1   2   3   4

Section 2

When someone cuts me off on the road, I fly into a rage and make sure they know it.

    1   2   3   4

Sometimes I get so upset that I lose control, hit things, or look for something to throw.

    1   2   3   4

I know God blessed me earlier, but my question is, where is He now?

    1   2   3   4

I can't hear God and I don't want to because of a mistake that I have made.

    1   2   3   4

I don't know why God requires so much of me and I have to do everything.

    1   2   3   4

I don't know why everyone wants something from me.

    1   2   3   4

I constantly ask questions like, why?

    1   2   3   4

If someone pushes my button, they will be sorry.

    1   2   3   4

I can't handle it if I think someone is making fun of me.

    1   2   3   4

It may sound strange, but I secretly agree with the radicals who bomb abortion clinics.

    1   2   3   4

In a life or death situation, I would not help someone who took another's life.

    1   2   3   4

Secretly, I do not like people of another skin color.

    1   2   3   4

I believe that people of my skin color are being constantly mistreated.

    1   2   3   4

I have a chip on my shoulder when it comes to race or gender.

    1   2   3   4

If someone opposes me, I swiftly put them in their place.

    1   2   3   4

No one is going to tell me the speed limit – I'll drive like I want to, as fast as I please.

    1   2   3   4

You'll get what you want if you are bold enough to get in someone else's face.

    1   2   3   4

Section 3

I really don't see anything wrong with watching soap operas.- watching the news is worse.

    1   2   3   4

If the opposite sex pulls their car next to mine, I smile and flirt just a little.

    1   2   3   4

I like the feeling that the opposite sex finds me attractive.

    1   2   3   4

I like the feeling of being wanted, so I tease the opposite sex.

    1   2   3   4

I believe if you are unmarried and really love someone, it's okay with God to have sex.

    1   2   3   4

I find myself talking to others of the opposite sex because my mate doesn't understand me.

    1   2   3   4

I truly don't believe unmarried sex is wrong because God gave me these desires.

    1   2   3   4

I don't believe that getting my needs met through pornographic material is wrong.

    1   2   3   4

I don't believe it's wrong to watch pornographic videos – I'm not the one doing it!

    1   2   3   4

I find myself sneaking on the Internet to view x-rated websites.

    1   2   3   4

I enjoy reading sensual novels.

    1   2   3   4

I secretly believe that sexual fantasies are fine because they don't hurt anyone.

    1   2   3   4

God created me with a beautiful body and I believe He wants me to show it off.

    1   2   3   4

I have sexual fantasies about a person I am not married to

    1   2   3   4

I've always been curious to go into a porno shop just to see what's in there.

    1   2   3   4

I don't see anything wrong with gay/lesbian lifestyles – to each his own.

    1   2   3   4

I don't see anything wrong with a teasing sexual remark made to the opposite sex.

    1   2   3   4

Section 4

I will never forget what a certain person did to hurt me.

    1   2   3   4

I've been hurt in this area before and if another person gets close, I withdraw.

    1   2   3   4

I hope a certain person gets exactly what I feel he deserve.

    1   2   3   4

I secretly believe that every preacher is the same – they all want your money.

    1   2   3   4

I believe that sometimes you have a right to hold a grudge.

1   2   3   4

If I am offended, I believe that I have the right to get even.

1   2   3   4

I have frequent headaches and usually have stomach problems.

1   2   3   4

I looked in the mirror and was surprised at how sad I looked.

1   2   3   4

If I get in an argument, the best thing to do is act like it never happened – no apologies.

1   2   3   4

I'm not sure I could ever be actively involved with a church again.

1   2   3   4

I don't tell people anything because all they do is talk about it to everyone else.

1   2   3   4

If I could live far away from human beings, I would be happy.

1   2   3   4

I feel like everyone uses me in order to get something else that they want.

    1   2   3   4

I don't know why I even try because it never turns out like I want it to.

    1   2   3   4

It doesn't do any good to talk about it, so I just tuck it away in my heart.

    1   2   3   4

If I had a better childhood, I would be a better person.

    1   2   3   4

Sometimes I don't think I ever had a chance.

    1   2   3   4

Take each section and tally your score. Check your results under each section.

Section 1 - PRIDE

If you scored

68 to 34 points: You have a strong spirit of pride that is hindering your life and you must give this area immediate attention.

33 to 18 points: You are dealing with pride and you need to stop the influence of it in your life – now!

To understand how detrimental pride is, we must understand that the attribute of it is directly opposite from the attributes of heaven. That would make pride totally satanic. Heaven is run by submission, obedience, and humility. The greatest person in the kingdom of God is not measured by how much the person does or accomplishes, but by how much of a servant's heart the person has. Greatest with God is determined by the person's ability to humble himself and be submissive, serving others. Anyone can take pride in themselves and what they do – that is not a sign of greatness. However, it takes great strength and shows greatness when a person can dedicate his or her life to serving God and others. Jesus was our prime example by showing us that the greater our ministry is, the more we will serve. Read and study James 4:6; Matthew 5:3; Philippians 2:5-8; Isaiah 14:12; Proverbs 6:16, 17; 28:25; 16:18; 11:2; 13:10; 29:23.

Section 2 – ANGER

If you scored

68 to 34 points: A strong spirit of anger is attempting to destroy your life and influence.

33 to 18 points: You are also dealing with anger and if left unchecked, it could prove detrimental to your life, your family, and your calling.

Contrary to the world, anger is not a demonstration of power and strength. Heaven views unharnessed anger as a lack of control and weakness as it results from our sinful nature. There is a righteous anger, but it can turn into sin if not directed in the right way. We need a holy hatred for sin, and anger should be directed in that channel – not against others. When it comes to anger, the enemy can get a foothold when we have not judged ourselves in two areas: (1) rights that we have not surrendered to God and (2) unchangeable irritations. Our lives will be at peace when we surrender our rights to the Lord and make allowances for things that we cannot change. Study these scriptures and allow the Holy Spirit to give you the under-standing and the strength to change. Proverbs 14:29; 16:32; 19:19, 22; Job 5:2; Job 19:29; Psalm 25:5; Matthew 11:29; Ephesians 6:4.

Section 3 – IMMORALITY

If you scored

68 to 34 points: The spirit of immorality is sabotaging your life and could destroy your family and your ministry. Seek out a trusted and mature Christian friend and get help now.

33 to 18 points: You are playing with something that is big-ger than you realize. Allow the Holy Spirit to convict your heart and open your eyes to the danger around you so you can be set free from immorality.

Only by developing a pure heart can we overcome moral impurity. When we grasp a revelation of Who the Holy Spirit wants to be in our lives we will then desire to separate from sin and consecrate ourselves to God. Our attitude toward sin has been more self-centered instead of God-centered, meaning that we don't consider something a sin if we like doing it. We should take God at His Word and call sin for what it is – then groom ourselves to be molded and changed by His Spirit so we won't desire any part of sin. God did not call us to be "cultural-ly holy." He called us to be like Him. If you have found your-self to be in frequent depression, it is probably a result of this spirit working against the nature of God within you. Decide today that you will follow righteousness, faith, love, and peace, and develop a clear conscience before the Lord. Read the following scriptures and make a decision – today – to live the life Jesus died and resurrected to give you. I Corinthians 6:12-20; Matthew 6:22, 23; 2 Timothy 2:22; I Timothy 5:22.

Section 4 – BITTERNESS

If you scored

68 to 34 points: You have opened a door to the enemy through unforgiveness and now bitterness is in your heart and soul. Your physical health is probably being afflicted and you are very sad most of the time.

33 to 18 points: You have unforgiveness in your life and are in danger of being overcome by the spirit of bitterness.

The Bible tells us to guard our hearts at all costs because from it, the issues of life flow out from us to others. Jesus told us that offenses would come. However, the offenses, the hatred, and the wars are not the problems He was concerned about. Jesus told us to guard our hearts against these things – so the heart is the key. As long as we are in the world, offenses will come. As long as you live, hurt will knock on your door. The key is not to allow it into your heart, but to forgive and hand it over to the Lord. To prepare your life as a servant and an armorbearer, you have to give up the spirit of revenge, forgive others the way the Lord has forgiven you, to see past the offense and into the heart of another, and to realize that forgiveness is the demonstration of true love and greatness. Allow the Holy Spirit to minister His grace and His love to you. Read these scriptures and determine to forgive and release all those who have offended you. Luke 17:1; Hebrews 12:14, 15; James 3:14, 15; Matthew 18:1-17; 6:12-15; Mark 11:25; Romans 12:18-21; 1 Corinthians 4:12, 13.

Part Two

–1–

The Hour of the Local Church

God is calling many Christians to become armorbearers for their leaders and for each other. We should begin to work as a team to advance God's kingdom in the earth. Think what would happen in this nation if people would get on fire for God and begin to release their gifts and talents in the Body of Christ! We would see the world reached with the Gospel. The local church is called to reach its community, town, city, or region for God. The church will succeed as people release their gifts and talents into the Body and the community.

1. From The Amplified Version or from the scripture written in Chapter 11, write out First Peter 4:10.

   _____

   _____

   _____

   _____

2. Now write First Peter 4:10 in your own words.

   _____

   _____

   _____

3. How have you used your gifts and talents in the local church?

_____

_____

_____

4. Do you see other gifts and talents developing within you? What are they?

_____

_____

_____

5. How can these gifts and talents be used for the Body of Christ and in your church?

_____

_____

_____

6. Fill in the blank. "Each Christian has a _____ on his life which will become _____ once he is _____ in a _____."

7. Is there a particular ministry that you would like to start in your local church?

_____

_____

_____

8. Have you followed these steps to begin it?_____

- Make certain the Holy Spirit is leading you to begin it.
- Make certain the Holy Spirit has confirmed it in prayer.
- Make a list of the steps you would do to begin it.
- Make a list of the scriptures you've found that validate this ministry.
- Take these items with you and discuss the new ministry with your pastor.
- Follow your pastor's instructions to begin the new ministry.

9. Of the 40 keys listed regarding Successful Keys to Blooming Where You Are Planted, list the 10 keys that ministered the most to you.

_____

_____

_____

_____

_____

_____

_____

_____

_____

_____

10.What are the four categories that we must understand so that we can bloom where we are planted?

A. _____

B. _____

C. _____

D. _____

–2–

Keys to Longevity

A.

1. The first key to longevity is:

_____

_____

2. The word longevity means, "long life."1 How does that definition relate to serving as an armorbearer?

_____

_____

3. Read Matthew 13:37, 38. What does it mean when God describes us as His "good seed?"

_____

_____

4. Genesis 1:11 says that the "seed is in itself." How does that relate to us as workers in the kingdom of God?

_____

_____

5. How will you know that your seed has come forth? What must you do?

_____

_____

6. If a tree is continually uprooted and replanted, eventually the roots will die. How does this relate to a Christian?

_____

_____

7. In this chapter, I cite one verse as being very important in understanding your calling. What is that scripture reference?_____

8. Write that verse.

_____

_____

9. What does that verse say to you?

_____

_____

10. Read Ephesians 5:27. The glorious Church refers to special people with a specific purpose. How does that scripture apply to you in this end time generation?

_____

_____

Will You Give Account?

11. Circle the correct answer whether true (T) or false (F). Answers are in the back of the book.

A. Not everyone will appear before the Judgment Seat of Christ.

   T   F

B. First Corinthians 5:10 tells us who will appear.

    T   F

C. My pastor can answer for me regarding how I used my gifts.

    T   F

D. God will give me some slack if I was a good mate and a good parent.

    T   F

E. We must be determined to have God's will in our lives no matter the cost.

    T   F

F. Sometimes it will take strong crying and many tears to stay where God plants you.

    T   F

G. Hebrews 5:7 tells us what Jesus went through to stay in the will of God.

    T   F

B.

1. Another priority for building longevity in your life is your _____

_____

2. Luke 11:1 is a very interesting scripture. In it we find that the disciples asked Jesus to teach them how to _____ but they never asked for His _____.

3. Many have fallen into sin because they _____
_____ of the _____ for an

_____ _____.

4. While in prayer one day, the Lord revealed to me keys to fulfilling the call. What are these four keys?

_____

_____

_____

_____

5. Explain the spiritual process of these four keys.

_____

_____

_____

_____

6. What is your first ministry?

_____

_____

_____

7. What was the key to Jesus' longevity?

_____

_____

C.

1. Another important part of longevity is _____ a
_____ and a _____.

2. Read Ecclesiastes 9:10 and write the verse here.

_____

_____

_____

3. Examine your life and ministry. What has your hand found to do in your local church?

_____

_____

_____

4. Can you do more? What is it? How will you begin?

_____

_____

_____

D.
1. Yet another key to longevity is _____

_____

_____

2. We must follow our _____ and not the _____.

3. God holds the future, and the _____ _____ for you does not always hold what seems to be the _____ _____.

E.

1. The fifth key to longevity is._____

2. Read Jeremiah 17:5-8. Now write those verses in your own words.

_____

_____

_____

3. If you lean toward man as your source, then man will be the _____ of your supply.

4. Your source of supply must be _____.

F.

1. Two other keys for longevity are _____ and _____

2. Read First Corinthians 15:10. What was the Apostle Paul saying in this verse?

_____

_____

_____

3. What then, does "grace" mean to you?

_____

_____

_____

4. Does 1 Corinthians 15:10 mean we can earn blessings based upon our works? Explain why?

_____

_____

_____

5. How has grace helped you in a particular situation?

_____

_____

_____

G.

1. _____ is another key to longevity and it means enduring without murmuring or fretting.2

2. What is the definition for patience given in the book?

_____

_____

_____

3. Why do many of our problems come?

_____

_____

_____

You Choose

Choose the letter that fits the best answer.

4. God wants to _____ first before He exalts your ministry.

a. Abundantly prosper you

b. Develop His character in you

c. Save your mate

d. Pay off your mortgage

5. Most of us like promotion first and _____ later.

a. Prosperity

b. Hard work

c. A big office

d. Character

6. As you determine to have the will of God in your life and get connected to a local church, the opportunities to _____ will be there.

a. Minister

b. Murmur, complain, and become impatient

c. Have dinner with the pastor

d. Go golfing with the pastor and staff

7. If you are in a difficult situation but you are assured that God called you there, He is probably _____.

a. Not listening to you.

b. Going to see that you get a raise.

c. Wanting you to take over the church.

d. Teaching you patience.

8. It is by _____ that you will receive the promise.

a. The word of the pastor

b. Faith and patience

c. Paying off your credit cards

d. Listening to your mate

9. Along with patience, you must have _____.

a. Flexibility

b. A box of Kleenex

c. A bottle of antacid

d. A tank full of gas and a road map

10. If you are not willing to change, you can easily get _____ and miss the prompting of the Holy Spirit.

a. Tunnel vision

b. A promotion

c. Acid reflux

d. A tank full of gas and a road map

11. Your life and ministry will stop dead in its tracks if you _____.

a. Use the charge cards

b. Watch CNN

c. Embrace someone who believes differently than you

d. Do not accept change

12. Acts 13:36 states that David "served his own generation by the will of God." List the ways that this generation thinks differently than the past generations (the sixties, seventies, eighties, and nineties).

_____

_____

13. How has the change in thinking over the past generations motivated your ministry as an armorbearer? As a minister? As a believer?

_____

_____

_____

14. What can you do to make sure that you are in tune with the way this generation thinks?

_____

_____

_____

–3–

Keys to Commitment

A.

1. The first key to commitment is a _____ and _____ that goes beyond all personal feelings.

2. List the four characteristics of a faithful man and write out the scriptures pertaining to them:

a. Proverbs 11:13

_____

_____

_____

b. Proverbs 13:17

_____

_____

_____

c. Proverbs 14:5

_____

_____

_____

d. Proverbs 20:6

_____

_____

_____

3. According to Chapter 9, how does the dictionary define loyalty?

_____

_____

_____

4. Faithfulness?

_____

_____

_____

5. Read First Corinthians 4:2. How can you be found faithful?

_____

_____

_____

B.

1. Another key to commitment is:

_____

_____

_____

2. There are spiritual laws that work for masters and servants alike. List three of those spiritual laws and the scriptures validating them.

a. _____

_____

_____

Scripture: _____

_____

b. _____
_____
_____

Scripture: _____
_____

c. _____
_____
_____

Scripture: _____
_____

3. Was there ever a time you felt too small to do something big? When was that time and what did you do about how you felt?

_____
_____
_____

4. Sometimes we can miss God because we see more _____ and we are_____.

5. When you are given more responsibility, how do you handle it?

_____
_____
_____

6.What are the ways you could handle this responsibility more efficiently?_____

_____

_____

_____

7. It is always God's plan to exalt you, but you will find you

_____

_____

_____

C.

1. Another key to commitment is symbolized this way: We must commit to the ministry as we are committed to

_____

_____

_____

2. Circle the correct answer whether true (T) or false (F).

a. Your marriage comes before your position in the church.
   T   F

b. You should approach the ministry with a similar commitment as your marriage.
   T   F

c. The same keys you apply to your marriage you should apply to the ministry.
   T   F

d. Communication is important in marriage; it is equally important in the ministry.

T   F

e. You won't have an effective ministry without communication.

T   F

f. Pastors must communicate as well as they expect their staff to communicate.

T   F

g. People must commit to the pastor, as well as the pastor committing to the people.

T   F

h. If a pastor is truly joined to the flock as a shepherd, the sheep will know his voice.

T   F

D.

1. Chapter 9 mentions three finals keys to commitment. What are they?

a. _____

b. _____

c. _____

2. Read Colossians 3:23, 24. How are these verses a reality in your life?

_____

_____

_____

3. What could you change in your life that would make "working unto the Lord and not unto men" a reality for you?

_____

_____

_____

4. What person(s) in the Bible is an inspiration to you as far as working as unto the Lord? Why is that and what did the person(s) do?

_____

_____

_____

Avoiding Burn Out

5. It's easy to say that spirit-filled Christians, especially ones in leadership, should never burn out. But the truth is, burn out is a combination of physical, emotional, and mental exhaustion that goes unattended by rarely taking the time to rest and refresh. The ministry is very demanding and working in the ministry is a lifestyle – the hours and the effort go far past the familiar 9 to 5. Burn out affects many of those in ministry, and often times, their decisions are a reflection of it.

As an armorbearer, you will always be on the front line of the ministry work. It is important that you find ways – even if they are small – to rest and refresh yourself. As much as possible, you should find ways that will take the pressure and exposure off of your leader and encourage them to refresh and rest them selves.

Take the test below and rate yourself from 1 to 4 (1 being

the lowest and 4 being the highest) to see how close you are to burn out. At the end of the test we'll discuss the methods to overcome the potential for future burn out.

I've noticed that my energy has been low and I am always tired.

    1   2   3   4

Although I am tired, I still have trouble sleeping at night.

    1   2   3   4

To ease my sleepless nights, I've turned to sleeping aids or prescription drugs.

    1   2   3   4

I've noticed that I have an increased susceptibility to illnesses (colds, flu, etc.)

    1   2   3   4

I've really been a "klutz" lately, very prone to accidents and carelessness.

    1   2   3   4

I've been extremely forgetful. I have trouble remembering the smallest things.

    1   2   3   4

I fight feelings of depression, hopelessness, and an inability to cope with reality.

    1   2   3   4

I feel like I've lost control and can't seem to get it back.

    1   2   3   4

People say I'm very irritable and touchy.

    1   2   3   4

I've found that I tend to be more nervous than I used to be.

    1   2   3   4

My family and friends have become just another demand on my life.

    1   2   3   4

I've turned cynical about my work.

    1   2   3   4

I have a negative attitude towards people that I work with.

    1   2   3   4

I have a "don't care" attitude about life.

    1   2   3   4

I feel overwhelmed and wish I were in a less demanding line of ministry.

    1   2   3   4

I am entertaining the idea of leaving the ministry but I am trapped due to money and status.

    1   2   3   4

Jesus seems very far away right now. I can't hear Him at all and I wonder what He thinks of me.

    1   2   3   4

What was your total score?

If you circled a "3" or a "4" on four or more of the statements, you are in the beginnings of a burn out. Even if you circled more than four, you can recover if you pay attention to your condition. Remember, the call of God upon your life – and your future – can suffer if you don't take care of yourself. Here are some suggestions to rid your life of burn out and to keep it from happening again.

1. Take inventory.

Get away. Do something or go to an environment that is relaxing to you and eases your mind. Then begin to reassess the environment you came out of. Examine then analyze the negative things that cause stress in your life and ministry and determine what can be done about it. Begin to establish those plans or guidelines. In the future, don't wait until you get burned out to take care of negative stressors. Learn to settle it at the first sign of symptoms.

2. Keep things in their place.

See life as a "compartment." Don't bring the problems of the ministry home with you and vice versa. If ministry problems need to be discussed at home, set aside a time to do so in advance. The ministry will always be a major part of your life, but the problems don't have to be. Keep your family time separate from the needs and wants of the people.

3. Acknowledge your weaknesses.

You can't do everything and you can't be everything to everyone. Make a list of the things that take the most of your time – things that someone else could do in your place and be as effective. If you don't have a person like that, then pray for your "Joshua" and begin training the person when he/she comes. We all have to do things we don't necessarily enjoy, but try to do more of what you enjoy and less of what you don't. Someone may be waiting to get the change to do the tasks you dislike.

4. Make time to relax.

Take time after work to do something that seems impractical. You may not think you have time to jog, run, or walk, but it will amaze you at how refreshed you will be if you'll take the time to do it. Force your mind to stop thinking about the events of the day and to slow down. The work will still be there tomorrow – in fact, it will always be there. Go get an ice cream cone. Maybe taking a long, hot shower, a visit to the hot tub or sauna, listening to music, reading, or even watching a movie could be the non-productive, relaxing answer to a very productive day. If God illustrated rest on the seventh day and Jesus rested, you need to follow Their example!

5. Look at what you've accomplished.

When the week is over, look at what you have done instead of what is left to do. Looking at what has been done encourages you and inspires you to tackle what is still left to do – later. Present what you've done to the Lord and ask for His wisdom and direction to complete the rest of the task. Then, like the Apostle Paul, press on to the mark of the high calling in Christ Jesus!

Remember, you only have one life to live on this earth and

one chance to live it. Take care of yourself so that you can be your best for the Lord and represent Him in true fashion. You are a special and chosen treasure to God, and taking care of yourself honors Him and His love for you.

6. God is preparing you for leadership. The key is to
_____ _____ to _____, your
_____, and the _____ set over you.

7. If you are truly committed to the church and pastor where God has sent you, then you
_____ when you face hard times.

8. The only way to succeed is to never _____.

–4–

Keys to Attidude

A.

1. The first key to attitude is a _____
_____ because this is what
leader's look for in people who desire to get involved.

2. You may not think you have the talent or ability to do
whatever is asked, but you will set yourself to do it
_____ you were asked.

3. Read Isaiah 1:19 and write out the verse.

_____

_____

_____

4. What does that scripture mean to you?

_____

_____

_____

5. Read First Chronicles 28:9. How does that scripture
apply to your life?

_____

_____

_____

B.

1. The next key to the right attitude is

_____

_____

_____

2. If you work on a ministry staff or in the ministry of helps, you must get a revelation of the _____ involved.

3. You must know that you are working for _____, loving _____, and daily giving your life for _____, all of whom God loves.

4. Without _____, there would be no

_____

5. If the best feeling you have about doing something in the ministry is "when it's over," why is your attitude wrong?

_____

_____

_____

6. Instead, what must your attitude be and what must you think?

_____

_____

_____

C.

1. A third key to having the right attitude is

_____

_____

_____

2. The victory begins with _____ because it is an attitude that will cause you to win in any situation.

3. What was the significant attitude that Paul represented in Philippians 1:15-19?

_____

_____

4. Read First Thessalonians 5:18. How does that scripture relate to your life?

_____

_____

_____

5. You may want a change in your life and position, but that will only come when you _____ to be _____ for _____ you are.

6. Read the story of Paul and Silas in Acts 16:23-26. From these scriptures and your imagination, list as many hardships as you can think of that these men were going through.

_____

_____

_____

7. How does their situation and what they chose to do in the midst of it, minister to you?

_____

_____

_____

8. When difficulties come to your life, how will you begin to be thankful in the midst of them?

_____

_____

_____

9. List the things you are thankful for.

_____

_____

_____

_____

10. Now make it a point to begin to thank God for those things each day and _____

D.

1. Jesus was a wonderful example of the next key to having a good attitude. What was this key?

_____

_____

2. Answer true (T) or false (F) by circling the correct answer. Answers are in the back of the book.

a. Christians will not always have to be servants. Promotion will come.

    T   F

b. Jesus told the disciples that those who were "chief" were the leaders.

    T   F

c. Elisha was recommended to the King of Judah because of the double anointing.

    T   F

d. David became king and had a great anointing because his father was well known.

    T   F

e. As you learn to delegate, the anointing of God will increase upon you to help others.

    T   F

3. Just as the sheep were with David, your "flock" is your

_____

4. Now, what is your flock?

_____

E.

1. God established chains of command under Him, meaning a key attitude for us is

_____

2. Read Romans 13:1, 2 and write what those verses say to you.

_____

_____

3. All _____ in authority are set up by God; the authority rests on the _____, not the _____.

4. In order to properly submit to authority, you must have a clear understanding that the _____

_____

5. What does the above statement mean when a difficulty arises? _____

_____

_____

6. Read Numbers 20:8-29. Now write what this story symbolizes today in those who misuse their office.

_____

_____

7. The only time we are not to submit to authority is when that authority directly violates the

_____

8. If an authority violates the Word of God, to whom do we submit? _____

9. If you begin to speak against your pastor or leaders because of rules that are not in violation to the Word of God.

_____

10. Answer true (T) or false (F) by circling the correct answer. Check your answers in the back of the book!

A. If God has sent you and they say, "That's how we do it here," you must still submit.

T   F

B. Rebellion usually starts over church rules, not violation of the Word of God.

T   F

C. If someone continually misuses an office, we can pray for him to change or get out.

T   F

D. If you have a problem, you need to talk to those in leadership in order to understand.

T   F

E. Heaven has a chain of authority.

T   F

11. Read Colossians 3:22, 23. What do these verses mean?

_____

_____

_____

12. There are five structures of authority that we all must submit to. They are:

a. _____

b. _____

c. _____

d. _____

e. _____

13. The first structure of authority is described in First John 2:3, 4. Explain why this authority is number one.

_____

_____

14. The second structure of authority is described in First Peter 2:13, 14. Explain these scriptures.

_____

_____

15. The third structure of authority is found in Hebrews 13:17. Explain this verse.

_____

_____

16. Ephesians 6:1 speaks of the fourth structure of authority. Explain this verse. Can you find other scriptures to validate this authority structure?

_____

_____

17. First Peter 2:18 describes the fifth authority structure. Explain how this verse speaks to the hearts of believers and their employers.

_____

_____

18. Authority is _____. We will never graduate from being _____.

19. When we go to heaven, we will still _____ to _____.

20. God will never graduate you to a _____ place of authority until you learn how to _____ to authority.

F.

1. The last key to maintaining a good attitude is

_____

_____

2. Read Proverbs 9:8, 9. Write out these verses.

_____

_____

_____

_____

3. According to these verses, if you are one who is going to rebuke, then be wise enough to _____ and_____.

4. What happens to a person if you just rebuke them and nothing more?

_____

_____

_____

5. God never assigned anyone to _____ a person's

_____.

6. On the other hand, if you are being the one rebuked, do not get your _____.

7. According to Scripture, how should one handle it if he is being rebuked?

_____

_____

_____

8. How do you personally handle a rebuke? (Be honest!)

_____

_____

_____

9. What can you do to better handle a rebuke?

_____

_____

_____

A Study In Proverbs

10. Read the following scriptures, write them out, and then explain their meaning.

A. Proverbs 12:15

_____

_____

B. To me, this scripture means

_____

_____

C. Proverbs 15:32

_____

_____

D. To me, this scripture means

_____

_____

E. Proverbs 19:25

_____

_____

F. To me, this scripture means

_____

_____

G. Proverbs 15:5

_____

_____

H. To me, this scripture means

_____

_____

11. We are told in the Bible to _____ ourselves
and make _____ when we need to
_____.

12. One of the reasons we are to submit to God-called leadership is so that we can be _____ to them
as they speak _____.

13. Remember: Stay _____ before the Lord, and when
you are _____, just _____ it and
_____ from it because there will be no growth
without some pruning.

–5–

Keys to Teamwork

A.

1. The first key to teamwork is _____

_____

_____

2. The main reason people leave churches is because

_____

_____

3. Did you ever leave a church over an offense? How has God ministered to you regarding that offense? How do you see it now in light of what the Holy Spirit has shown you?

_____

_____

_____

_____

4. Anyone can take offense, get hurt, and walk out, but it takes a _____ or _____ to make it _____.

5. The key to overcoming offense is found in Matthew 18:34, 35. What is the key?_____

B.

1. The next key to teamwork is _____

_____

2. Answer the following statements by writing True or False in the space provided. Answers are in the back of the book.

a. _____ Since the Church functions like a team, they need your talents and abilities.

b. _____ You have talents lying dormant, just waiting to be used.

c. _____ You can find those talents by faithfully serving and drawing on the Creator inside of you.

d. _____ Jesus is the One who distributes gifts and talents.

e. _____ You do not have a choice in the gifts or talents you have received.

f. _____ You will only be accountable for your own gifts and talents.

g. _____ If you can't play the drums and have no rhythm, you won't answer for that.

h. _____ The Spirit of God is saying loud and clear that it is time for us to release our gifts into the earth.

3. Read Matthew 25:13-15. Now read verse 35. What are these verses saying to us?

_____

_____

_____

4. Read First Peter 4:10. Now write out the verse. Can you say that you do not have any gifts or talents? Why not?

_____

_____

_____

C.

1. The last two keys to teamwork are _____ and learn to _____.

2. Read First Corinthians 12:12-15. Paul compares the members of the Body of Christ with the members of the physical body. With that in mind, why is the ministry of helps not a "second fiddle" position?

_____

_____

_____

3. If you are going to fulfill your part in the Body, you must stop looking at your _____ and start using your _____.

4. First Corinthians 1:10 and Acts 4:32 are two verses with a similar message. What is the similarity in meaning?

_____

_____

_____

5. If you are trying to run with a vision that God has not given your pastor, then you are going to create _____.

_____

Do you really want to do exploits for God? Are you willing to find your place in the Body and get connected with the other members of your local church? Are you ready to release the gifts and talents that Jesus has given to you and placed within you? If so, get involved with the local church. Serve the people and be an arm of the leadership. God will never force you to obey His will because He has given you the right to choose. We are all called to be armorbearers one for another. Just think what we could do in the earth if each person would pick up their mantle and take their place. Now is the time for you to join the ranks of God's great army – it's not too late. Trust God and allow Him to bring to pass the course He has chosen for you to walk. Allow Him to cultivate and bring forth the gifts and talents within you. You don't have to lean on your own understanding. It is God who directs your steps by making every crooked path straight. This is our generation and our day. We are the chosen of God, so let us rise up and be the army He has called us to be! We are the Church!

Part One

Chapter 1

Answers

1. *David*
2. a. Skillful in playing, b. mighty man of valor, c. a man of war, d. prudent (wise) in speech, e. handsome (well-groomed) person, f. The Lord was with him.
3. The generation is self-serving. Instead of offering to wait on others, we in the Church often expect people to wait on us.
4. Personal reflection
5. Judges 9:54, 1 Samuel 14:7, 12, 13, 14, 17; 16:21, 31:4, 5, 6; 2 Samuel 23:37; 1 Chronicles 10:4, 5; 11:39.
6. A. Nasa or Nacah and Keliy from the root word, kalah.
7. To lift.
8. Accept, advance, bear, bear up, carry away, cast, desire, furnish, further, give, help, hold up, lift, pardon, raise, regard, respect, stir up, yield.
9. To end.
10. Complete, consume, destroy utterly, be done, finish, fulfill, long, bring to pass, wholly reap, make clean riddance.
11. The duty of the armorbearer was to stand beside his leader to assist him, to lift him up, and to protect him against any enemy that might attack him.
12. Spirit of Christ. Heart of a servant.

Chapter 2

Answers

Questions on pages 13 an 14 are personal reflections.

First Duty

1. Strength. a. faith, peace. b. You must be able to stand

with your pastor and aid him through trials, tests, and difficulties as well as the victories. To do that, you will need spiritual maturity.

2. Joy, victory.

3. Physically, mentally, spiritually.

Second Duty

1. Respect, acceptance, tolerance, personality

1, 2, 3, 4, personal reflection

2. No. a. personal reflection. b. personal reflection

3. Determine that if the end result of the pastor's plan is to build and extend the Kingdom of God and win souls for Jesus, then it does not matter whose methods are used.

4. Goal, methods.

5. Personal Reflection

6. Argue, challenge, work with.

Third Duty

1. Thoughts.

2. a. F,
   b. F,
   c. F,
   e. T,
   f. T,
   g. T.

3. A. personal refelction
   B. personal reflection
   C. personal refelction
   D. personal reflection

Fourth Duty
1. Agreement, submission.
2. Write verses
3. Personal Reflection
4. Personal Reflection
5. All the answers are true.
6. Humility, meekness, forgiveness, purity, clear conscience.
7. a. humility — personal reflection
   b. meekness — personal reflection
   c. forgiveness — personal refelection
   d. purity — personal reflection
   e. clear conscience — personal reflection
8. d.
9. c.
10. b.
11. c.
12. a
13. a.
14. a.
15. d.

Fifth Duty
1. Advancement.
A. personal reflection

Sixth Duty
1. Thrust, press, force.
2. - 8 personal reflection
A. Thrust: "to push with sudden force;" Press: "steady force or weight;" Force: "strength, power, effectiveness."
2.
8. Personal reflection
Allow the Holy Spirit to minister to you, dance, praise,

worship (personal responses).
9. a.
10. b.
11. c.
12. c.
13. d.
14. d.

Seventh Duty
1. Immediately, correctly.
2. Personal reflections — quiz

Eighth Duty
1. Support.
2. "That which supports or upholds; a sustainer, a comforter, a maintainer, a defender."
3. They hurt, make mistakes, get frustrated, bothered, face discouragement, and disappointment.
4. Uphold, sustain, maintain, defend our leader, being there for him/her to lean on in times of need.
5. Yes. When they are concerned with only one thing, "What about me?"
6. To raise up the shield of faith and protect him/her from the harmful words of people and the fiery darts of the devil.
7. When you have first mastered the art of supporting your spiritual leader.

Ninth Duty
1. Communicator.
2. All the answers are true, EXCEPT the last one. It is false.

Tenth Duty
1. Disposition, victories.

2. Represent.
3. "Thy gentleness has made me great."
4. Personal reflection
5. Making the pastor look bad, putting the blame on the pastor, etc.
6. Heart of a shepherd.
7. Deal with them in love and find some common ground of agreement with the ones with whom you work and deal. No one is unreachable as long as they are teachable.
8. Humility, meekness, forgiveness, purity, a clear conscience.

Eleventh Duty
1. Strength, courage.
2. "Bravery; the ability to encounter difficulties and danger with firmness, boldness and valor."3
3. Personal reflection
4. a. 2 b. Joshua and Caleb.
5. Faith.
6. Word of God.
7. The false idea that the pastor is more concerned with fulfilling his own personal vision than he is with meeting the needs of his associates and staff members.
8. He would not have placed you in that ministry to begin with.
9. Waiting for us in heaven.
10. Attitude.

Chapter 3

Answers

1..Abimelech was laying siege to a city and winning when he came to a tower to take refuge and a woman threw down a millstone and cracked his skull. He asked his armorbearer to kill him so it wouldn't be said that a woman killed him.

2. Loyalty, faithfulness, concerned about his leader's tainted honor.

3. Saul and his army were fighting against the enemy and losing ground. Realizing that defeat was certain, as his army began to flee, Saul was wounded by arrows. He turned to his armorbearer and commanded him to kill him so the enemy would not capture him and torture him to death.

4. He probably had other plans to escape with Saul and almost certainly felt that Saul could have survived the wounds. The Bible says he feared Saul, meaning he had great honor and reverence for the king. His entire service was to care for the king and preserve him, so it was difficult, if not impossible for him to take Saul's life.

5. Saul fell on his own sword and committed suicide. His armorbearer then took his own life to follow in death the one he gave his life to protect.

6. Jonathan ordered his armorbearer to secretly go with him over to the enemy's garrison. God confirmed that He was with them and when Jonathan came into the enemy's camp, they fell before him and his armorbearer killed the ones that had fallen. The armorbearer was willing to follow Jonathan even on what appeared to be a whim.

7. He wins victories and slays enemies while his leader gets the glory; one who trusts his officer, even in what may appear to be a whim; one who takes his place behind the man he serves, not striving to get out in front.

8. Saul was very troubled, having a distressing spirit. He decided to find a skillful musician who could ease his mind when he was oppressed. A young man was recommended to him by one of his servants. The young man was David. David played his instrument and the evil spirit left Saul. Saul loved him greatly and David reverenced Saul. David became Saul's armorbearer.

9. Skillful in playing (doing the work); mighty man of valor (courageous); a man of war (spiritually mature); prudent in speech (wise communicator); handsome in appearance (well-groomed); One whom the Lord was with (the hand of the Lord was with him).

10 Because he had once been Saul's armorbearer and he had great respect and honor towards the Lord's anointed. It also explains his attitude of extreme sorrow, repentance, and humility before Saul when David cut off a portion of his robe in the cave.

Who's Who?

1. C

2. B

3. D

4. D

5. A

6. B

7. C

8. B.

Chapter 4

Answers

   A. T
   B. F
   C. T
   D. F
   E. T
   F. T
   G. T
   H. T
   I. T
   J. T
   K. T
   L. T
   M. T

2. A, B, C, D, E, F, Personal reflection
3. 3, 1, 4, 2.
4. Only statements B, E, and F are wrong. All others should have an "X."

Chapter 5

Answers

1. Personal refelction
2. Invest his experience, maturity, advice, and wisdom. Give him authority without fear.
3. God birthed the vision within the pastor. God is the One who finishes it. The work God has begun should continue long after the pastor is gone.
4. a. Pray, divinely-appointed; b. invest yourself; c. delegate, responsibility, authority; d. spirit, armorbearer.
5. General, army.

Chapter 6

Answers

1. a. Pride, b. anger, c. immorality, d. bitterness.
   pages 58-69 — personal reflection

Part Two

Chapter 1

Answers

1. Write out scripture
2. Personal reflection
3. Personal reflection
4. Personal reflection
5. Personal reflection
6. Call, apparent, involved, church.
7. Personal reflection
8. Personal reflection
9. Personal reflection
10. a. Longevity, b. commitment, c. attitude, d. teamwork.

Chapter 2

Answers

A.
1. Understanding the call of God.
2. Armorbearer ministry is not a stepping stone position. As long as God wills, you are in the position for life.
3. He has put His Spirit within us and "sowed" us into the earth to reap a harvest.
4. What we need is already inside of us. We just need to cultivate it by having an intimate relationship with the

Lord and by serving others.

6. You will see tangible results. If you are where God has called you and stay planted there even during the hard times, the seed will come forth.

7. No fruit can develop if a person jumps from church to church, running from trouble.

8. Second Timothy 1:9.

9. Write the verse

10. Personal reflection

11. God has raised up a people who will not compromise His Word, people with His Spirit, anointing, and joy to go forth in these end times, bringing the greatest move of God that the earth has ever seen.

12. a. F
    b. F
    c. F
    d. F
    e. T
    f. T
    g. T.

B.

1. Personal relationship with Christ.

2. Pray, anointing.

3. Substituted the work, ministry, intimate relationship.

4. Intimacy, pregnancy, travail, birth.

5. Intimate, personal relationship with God, pregnant with His vision, travail or pray and intercede it into manifestation, birth of the vision in the natural.

6. To worship and honor the Lord on a daily basis.

7. A habit of prayer.

C.

1. Having, vision, goal.

2. Write verse

3. Personal reflection
4. Personal reflection

D.
1. Knowing that you are in the ministry that God intends for you.
2. Hearts, offers.
3. Best future, best offer.

E.
1. Making God your complete Source.
2. Read verse, personal reflection
3. Limit.
4. God.

F.
1. Trust in God's grace on your life, always obey God's original instructions.
2. He was what he was by the grace (power) of God.
3. Personal reflection
4. No. We obey; God performs. No pressure, no works.
5. (Personal reflection)

G.
1. Patience.
2. "The suffering of afflictions, pain, toil, calamity, provocation, or other evil with a calm, unfurled temper."
3. We are not patient.
4. b
5. d
6. b
7. d
8. b

9. a
10. a
11. d
12. Personal insight, discussion
13. Personal reflection
14. Personal reflection, insight

Chapter 3

Answers

A.

1. Loyalty, faithfulness.
2. a. Knows how to keep his mouth shut, b. ministers strength to his pastor, c. always speaks the truth, d. is a humble man.
3. "Faithful to a prince or a superior, true to a plighted faith, duty, or love."
4. "Firmly adhering to a duty, loyal, true to one's allegiance."
5. By being watched as you serve.

B.

1. Don't ever be too big to do the small, but don't ever be too small to do the big.
2. a. Reap what you sow, Gal. 6:7, b. Pride brings a fall, Prov. 16:18, c. Unteachable spirit brings deception, Rom. 12:13.
3. Personal reflection
4. Responsibility, afraid we cannot handle it.
5. Personal reflection
6. Personal reflection
7. Will have to expand.

C.

1. Marriage.
2. The first answer is false. All the other answers are true.

D.

1. a. Do your best,
   b. stay with something until the job gets done,
   c. never quit or give up.
2. Personal reflection
3. Personal reflection
4. Personal reflection, discussion
5. Personal reflection
6. Stay committed, God, Call, Leaders.
7. Will not quit.
8. Quit.

Chapter 4

Answers

A.

1. Willingness to do whatever you are asked.
2. Because.
3. (Write verse)
4. (Personal reflection)
5. (Personal reflection)

B.

1. To never lose sight of the people behind the work.
2. People.
3. People, people, people.
4. People, churches.
5. Because you allowed yourself to get caught up in all of the work and responsibility. The focus was not upon people.

6. "Here is an opportunity to minister to more people and God is letting me have a part."

C.
1. Being thankful for your position and retaining your joy.
2. Thanksgiving.
3. Although he was being slandered, he was thankful that Christ was being preached to the lost.
4. (Personal reflection)
5. Learn, thankful, where.
6. Deepest cell, human waste, dampness, disease, rodents, darkness, smell of death, etc.
7. Personal reflection
8. Personal reflection
9. Personal reflection
10. Do it!

D.
1. He had a servant's heart.
2. a-e All of the answers are false.
3. Area of responsibility or proving ground.
4. Personal reflection

E.
1. Submitting to God's delegated authority.
2. Write verses, personal reflection
3. Offices, office, person.
4. Authority rests on the office.
5. You are to submit yourself to the office, not the person or personality.
6. If the office is misused, the person can be replaced.
7. True.
8. The higher authority – God.

9. Rebellion.
10. a-e All of the answers are true.
11. Jesus is the Eternal Employer – we work as unto Him.
12. a. God and His Word; b. national and local government; c. the church; d. the family; e. employers.
13. God and His Word are the highest authority.
14. Submit to every ordinance for the Lord's sake – IRS, taxes, city laws, etc.
15. Obey those who have rule over you, because they must answer for your souls.
16. Children should obey their parents for this is right.
17. Must be subject to employers, and not just the good ones. If the employer is evil, pray that God will change them.
18. Here to stay. Under authority.
19. Submit, authority.
20. Greater, submit.

F.

1. Being big enough to be rebuked and corrected.
2. Write out verses
3. Instruct, teach.
4. It amounts to criticism and results in nothing but wounds and strife.
5. Break, spirit.
6. Feelings hurt.
7. Take it and do not hold a grudge or be defensive.
8. Personal reflection
9. Personal reflection
10. Personal reflection
    A. write scripture
    B. Personal refelction
    C. Write scripture
    D. Personal reflection
    F. Personal reflection

G. Write scripture
H. Personal reflection
11. Judge, correction, change.
12. Accountable, into our lives.
13. Humble, corrected, receive, learn.

Chapter 5

Answers

A
1. Walking without offense.
2. They get offended.
3. (Personal reflection)
4. Real man, real woman, right.
5. Forgiveness.

B.
1. Using all your talents and abilities.
2. a-h all of the answers are True.
3. Personal reflection
4. Personal reflection

C.
1. To know that you are needed, rest in God and let Him lead you into the perfect plan for your life.
2. Just as the example of the liver being invisible, yet very vital to sustain life, so is the ministry of helps. The ministry of helps has a very vital position.
3. Inabilities, abilities.
4. One heart, one soul, to all speak the same thing.
5. Division.